Sophoetics:

Philosophy Poems

poems by

J. Martin Strangeweather

Finishing Line Press
Georgetown, Kentucky

Sophoetics:

Philosophy Poems

Copyright © 2023 by J. Martin Strangeweather
ISBN 979-8-88838-266-0 First Edition
All rights reserved under International and Pan-American Copyright Conventions. No part of this book may be reproduced in any manner whatsoever without written permission from the publisher, except in the case of brief quotations embodied in critical articles and reviews.

Publisher: Leah Huete de Maines

Editor: Christen Kincaid

Cover Art: J. Martin Strangeweather

Author Photo: J. Martin Strangeweather

Cover Design: Elizabeth Maines McCleavy

Order online: www.finishinglinepress.com
               also available on amazon.com

                    Author inquiries and mail orders:
                           Finishing Line Press
                             P. O. Box 1626
                      Georgetown, Kentucky 40324
                                U. S. A.

Table of Contents

Invocation to the Muses 1
Dear Self 2
Allegory of the Cave 3
Bracketing 4
The Postmodern Cogito 5
Words Speak Themselves 6
Fibonacci's Looking Glass 7
The Title of this Poem 8
Thus Wept Zarathustra 9
Black Jewish Lesbian 10
Never Trust a Nazi 11
The Pain Game 12
Modal Identity 13
Endless Web 14
The History of Philosophy 15
Building a Better Bomb 17
Phil 100: Introduction to Philosophy 18
Epistemology in Blue 20
Everyday Ontology 22
You Still Have 14,537 Bowel Movements to Go
    Before You're Done Here 23
Atom Bomb Buddhism 25
Mind = Matter 26
Focus 27
Objectively Subjective 28
The Philosopher's Stone 29
Domestic Warfare 30
Brain in a Vat 31
Heresy of an Honest Man 32
The Big Question 33
Three Little Answers 34
What Do I Really Want to Know? 35
Satori 36
Sharing a Moment with the Cleaning Lady 38
The Hypnotherapist 40
Cancellation Meditation 42

for Mary Rose,
you've taught me more about life and myself
than any book ever could

Invocation to the Muses

alternate title:
**Sometimes the Difference
Between Desperation and Inspiration
Is a Reputable Agent**

Beseeching the poesy wellsprings
For professional assistance
In my endeavor
To translate the cosmos within,
I filled out a ten-page request form
In triplicate,
Submitted the paperwork
To the proper functionaries
Along with a copy of my birth certificate
And a sample of my urine,
Then waited patiently for my turn.

They refused me.

Studious Clio was busy studying,
Musical Euterpe was performing at a concert,
Comedic Thalia laughed at my request,
Tragic Melpomene was too depressed
To get out of bed,
Gay Terpsichore was dancing at nightclubs
For the rest of the century,
Erotic Erato was running late for a date
With an author more famous than I,
Pensive Polyhymnia said she would get back to me
After she finished calculating *pi*.
Cosmic Urania had her head in the clouds
Mapping all the stars in the sky,
And queenly Calliope told me outright
That she would never deign
To associate her name
With this balderdash!

Dear Self

I am writing this for you
Who is currently me.

This is a message to my future self.

Consciousness flows inward
And outward.
Consciousness is observation
And creation.

I am writing this for me
Who is currently you.

This is a message from your past self.

Mind is memory
And emotion,
A sieve
And a cleaver.

All possibilities have been realized
And have yet to be realized
In the branching tree
Of infinity.

What shall we study this time around—
The sacred seed?
The unseen roots?
The sturdy trunk?
The chaotic branches?
The dying leaves?
The ripening fruit?

Listen to the chorus of birds…

Allegory of the Cave *(a villanelle)*

Down in the cave where the shackled souls dwell
You confuse torchlight for the sun
Casting shadows on the wall in the thrall of Plato's hell.

"You will find no exit here," says Sartre tolling the somber bell,
"No door, no lock, no key, no fun,"
Down in the cave where the shackled souls dwell.

Eyesight deceives you but not your sense of smell,
Though it reeks of sulfur everywhere, and your ears are overrun
With constant babble from the rabble in the pit of Plato's hell.

Everyone is your adversary as far as you can tell,
And the closest thing to freedom is the smoking barrel of a gun,
Down in the cave where the shackled souls dwell.

To the right of you is Sisyphus, on your left the brightest star that fell,
Row after endless row of mental spools unwound and mortal coils undone,
Grasping at flickers of truth with Tantalus in the dark of Plato's hell.

Reality down here is just a flimsy empty shell;
Whisperings of daylight are one of the rare conspiracies we shun
In the allegorical cave where our shackled souls dwell,
Where we live and die by the ingrained lies we incessantly buy and sell.

Bracketing

Husserl taught us
to suspend our judgement
of the objective world,
and embrace the experience
of ourselves;
not to see the world
as illusion, hallucination, or dream,
but to see the world
as it presents itself.

The Postmodern Cogito

Do I think? What if I'm a program in a computer simulation? Do programs in computer simulations think? Do computers think, or merely simulate thinking? Is the simulation of thinking the same as thinking? I think therefore I am… I am what? Am I even me? It's possible I think, therefore it's possible I exist… but only like a thought or a dream or a group hallucination.

In my collectively authored experience of the world, the simulation referred to as "I" is psychosocially programmed to simulate the definition of thinking, which my psychosocial programming correlates with the requirement for the definition of existing. But what does a simulation know aside from what it's been programmed to know? Does programming constitute knowing?

I seem to think (even though I can't fully define what thinking means), therefore I seem to exist (even though I can't fully define what existence means).

Maybe I only exist if *you* think I exist.

Words Speak Themselves

Symbols are aliens come to conquer.
Symbols are doppelgangers come to replace.
Symbols are zombies come to infect.

Socrates was distrustful of the written word, according to the writings of Plato.

Let the words flow into you.
Let the words flow out from you.
The words are you.

The words speak through you, and wherever words end, so do you.

Fibonacci's Looking Glass

Form
constrains
and directs,
focusing our minds
to see beyond the mirror
which surrounds us and holds us all captive
to our very own gaze,
a guiding spirit
or ghost
given
flesh.

**The Title of This Poem
Is
This Poem Has No Title
Except
The Title of This Poem
Is
This Poem Has No Title
And
This Is the Poem**

Thus Wept Zarathustra

Last man, last man,
When did you give up hope?

It happened once I realized
A fire is burning
At both ends
Of my tightrope.

Overman, overman,
Where did your will to power go?

It was stolen by crooked crosses
Whose skin is white as snow,
But their blood
Is black as oil.

Go around, come around,
Merry-go-round these lifetimes flow,
Sorrow ever raining gentle teardrops,
Under which fools ever pray love will grow.

Nietzsche, Nietzsche,
Did you bite off the snake's head
And swallow it whole?

You said God is dead,
But your mind is sacred flame
And your brain a brass bowl.

Black Jewish Lesbian

I wanted to study ethics, so they told me to read Plato, who was an advocate of slavery. My ancestors were slaves.

I wanted to study ethics, so they told me to read Aristotle, who believed women were deformed men. I am a woman. They also told me to read Hegel, who believed women weren't intelligent enough to study philosophy, and Schopenhauer, who believed women were barely smarter than animals.

I wanted to study ethics, so they told me to read Augustine, who believed homosexuality was immoral. I am a lesbian.

I wanted to study ethics, so they told me to read Descartes, who believed animals were unfeeling machines. I am a vegetarian.

I wanted to study ethics, so they told me to read Kant, who believed whites were superior to blacks. I am black.

I wanted to study ethics, so they told me to read Heidegger, who was a member of the Nazi party. I am Jewish.

Never Trust a Nazi

Heidegger was a Nazi.
They say he was a great thinker,
But seriously,
How can you be a great thinker
If you're a Nazi?

The Pain Game

Is pain what I feel
when I believe I'm in pain?
Must I believe in pain
to feel it?
Am I feeling the pain
or the belief?

Is the painful feeling
my nervous system alerting me to tissue damage,
or could it be the memory of a painful experience
grafted onto a similar experience I'm currently experiencing?
Is my pain a trained response,
a learned set of behaviors?

If I'm in pain, do I only recognize it
through a desire
to alleviate the unwelcome sensation?
Is my pain physically real,
or just in my mind?

The answer is always yes, and sometimes no.

Modal Identity

There is something it is like to be tired.
There is something it is like to be thirsty.
There is something it is like to be sad.

There is something it is like to breathe underwater through gills.
There is something it is like to soar through the air on feathered wings.
There is nothing it is like to be a fish or a bird.

There is nothing it is like to be human.

There is something it is like to read this sentence with a firm grasp of the English language, whether you are a human, a Martian, an artificially intelligent computer, or an intellectually enhanced chimpanzee.

Endless Web

You have a concept of life
    that you correlate with a concept of death
            that you correlate with a concept of afterlife
        that you correlate with a concept of justice
that you correlate with a concept of truth
          that you correlate with a concept of identity
    that you correlate with a concept of history
    that you correlate with a concept of memory
            that you correlate with a concept of mind
    that you correlate with a concept of brain
that you correlate with a concept of body
      that you correlate with a concept of physicality
          that you correlate with a concept of physics
    that you correlate with a concept of math
      that you correlate with a concept of proof
     that you correlate with a concept of belief
    that you correlate with a concept of causality
that you correlate with a concept of time,
and so on…
but are you the spider or the fly?

The History of Philosophy

Confucius said all is order seeking harmony.
Buddha said all is delusion & desire.
Thales said all is water.
Heraclitus said all is fire.
Anaximenes said all is air.
Democritus said all is earth, in the form of atoms.
Empedocles said all is governed by the fundamental forces of love & strife.
Parmenides said all is timeless & immutable.
Pythagoras said all is math & music.
Socrates said all is shadow play.
Plato said all is divine geometric ideation.
Aristotle said all is logical.
Schopenhauer said all is irrational.
Bergson said all is two senses of time: segmented clock time & continuous duration.
Augustine said all is two modes of time: mortal linear time & God's omnitemporality.
Aquinas said all was initially caused by the Uncaused Cause, or God.
Kierkegaard said we are personally responsible for all of our choices & beliefs.
Ockham said all is elegantly simple.
Lorenz said all is chaotically complex.
Descartes said all is two distinct substances: mental & material.
Hobbes said all is matter.
Berkeley said all is mind,
Much of which Freud said is subconscious,
Much of which Jung said is the collective unconscious.
Wittgenstein said all is language.
Wiener said all is information.
Russel said all things are knowable.
Kant said all things in themselves are unknowable.
Hume said all things are uncertain.
Sartre said all things are what you make of them.
Derrida said all things are inexhaustibly analyzable.
Hegel said all is the dialectical synthesis of thesis & antithesis.
Marx said all is socioeconomic power play.
Nietzsche said all is will to power.
Einstein said all is deterministic.

Bohr said all is random.
What do *you* say?
It's still up for debate…

Building a Better Bomb

"Wake up, dear. It's time to go to school."
"Aw, I don't wanna."
"But you have to, dear. You're the teacher."

The words are dead. The sentences came out stillborn, no doubt about that. The only lively passages are the plagiarized ones. The teacher looks at the clock. It's only been ten minutes. He looks at the stack of essays. A disheveled tower of incompetence waiting to ruin his weekend, hundreds of pages scrawled with graffiti, tattooed with text. He looks at the students. Their bored boring faces remind him of how long he had to attend college just to babysit the future inmates of Folsom. Babysitting body bags. Babysitting dust. He looks at the clock. It's only been two minutes since the last time he looked. He looks at the students. Their spaded hands thrust upward like fascist salutes, anxious to ask him a question he has no interest in answering. He looks at the clock. Its hands are refusing to move. He looks at the students. Their blooming pimples and budding sources of shame awkwardly remind him of all the rites of passage he missed out on while struggling to maintain a 3.3 GPA in high school. He looks at the clock. It's frowning 8:20 at him. He looks at the students, wondering if they can tell he has a hangover.

Teacher teacher, burning bright…

Phil 100: Introduction to Philosophy

Having a philosophy
and doing philosophy
are two very different things.
Most of us think our Philosophy 100 course is devoted
to arguing with the professor,
but it also teaches us how to argue in general.
He questions everything we say,
and everything we *don't* say,
teaching us to question the use of terms such as
belief,
truth,
justice,
morality,
causality,
love,
life,
death,
time,
past,
present,
future,
infinity,
god,
soul,
mind,
consciousness,
subconsciousness,
spirit,
body,
world,
universe,
reality,
and so on,
redefining words that most of us take for granted,
or outright abolishing their acceptability
in intelligible discourse.
Words are no longer words to us.

We're trained to perceive them as linguistic operations
that are often misused.
"Language is the alchemical algebra one implements
to transform reality into one's own image,"
the professor has us recite at the beginning of every class.
"The world comes to life through our desires and expectations,
and without our desires and expectations
there is no world."
His dialectical methodology
for finding loopholes, redundancies, and contradictions
in anything we believe
is thoroughly incontrovertible.
During his class,
there is no such thing as Truth with a capital **T**
hiding behind the evolving rules of our made-up games.
There are only perspectives, POVs,
all of which are shortsighted.
He handed back our midterms today.
Nobody received higher than a C+,
but we know the grades don't really matter.

Epistemology in Blue

Who taught me
How to feel
Like I'm never okay
Like I'm never satisfied

Could it have been mass media?

Who taught me
How to think
That I'll never have enough
That I'll never be enough

Could it have been school?

Who taught me to be distrustful
Who taught me to be vengeful

Could it have been everyone I ever loved?

Who taught me to lie
Who taught me to pretend

Could it have been all of my family and friends?

Who taught me to feel nervous
Who taught me to feel scared

Could it have been you, dear reader?

My blues are red with rage
Which is why I speak so purple
Like a bruise

We are sermons
Waiting alone at the bus stop
In the rain

We are lessons
Overcrowded to indecipherability
Blurring through the subway

Our secrets keep secrets from us
Careful what you teach, brothers and sisters
"Amen!" cries a chorus of devils

Everyday Ontology

"I'm gonna go offer that bum the other half of my sandwich."

"You shouldn't call them bums," says my activist friend, looking at me with horror. "He doesn't have a home, so he's a homeless person. That's how you should refer to him."

"Fine, I'm gonna go offer that homeless person the other half of my sandwich."

"You shouldn't call him a homeless person," says my overreactivist friend, looking at me with disgust, as if he didn't just tell me otherwise. "You need to be more careful with your words."

"But you just said—"

"He's an unhoused individual."

"What's the difference?"

"Homeless means he doesn't have a home, implying he doesn't have any sort of family or roots. Unhoused simply means he doesn't have a house. It's like that one song says: *Papa was a rolling stone, wherever he laid his hat was his home.*"

"Whatever you say, bud. I'm gonna go offer that unhoused individual the other half of my sandwich now, if that's okay with you."

"You shouldn't call him an unhoused individual," says my redactivist friend, growing very annoyed with me. "He's an urban nomadic citizen with an on-the-go lifestyle!"

"When you put it that way, I'm almost envious."

"Is homelessness a joke to you?"

"Don't you mean unhousedness?"

You Still Have 14,537 Bowel Movements to Go Before You're Done Here

What if I was able to predict the future, and I knew things about you, things you yourself didn't know? What if I knew you were going to die in your mid-seventies? To be precise, what if I knew your whole life would amount to the sum of 27,301 days, or about 3,900 weeks? What if I knew you had 72 times left to make love to your spouse? Or worse, what if I knew you only had 10 times left? What if I knew you will hug your child 46 more times before parting ways forever? What if I knew the last time you hugged your mom was the last time you will ever hug her?

You only have so many times
To fight,
To cry,
To feel the beauty of sadness.

What if I knew 2,136 weeks of your time here will be spent feeling bad in one way or another, and you'll spend about 11,000 hours being sick? What if I knew the last 16 days of your life will be a waking nightmare? Should I tell you? Would you even want to know? What would you do with such knowledge?

You only have so many times
To laugh,
To dance,
To dream of silver linings.

There are only so many words left in you.
Spend them wisely.

There are only so many
Books,
Movies,
Video games,
Rainbows,
Occasions to hold someone's hand
Left in you.

This is a soup can sentiment
Elevated to the level of high art.
You've heard these words
Many times before,
Sometimes issuing from your own mouth.
You know these words,
But sometimes knowing isn't enough.

The term YOLO should be less about
Skydiving and bungee jumping,
And more about compassion and forgiveness.

The saddest thought in the world
Is that you might never get another chance
To say I'm sorry
Or…
I love you.

Atom Bomb Buddhism

The first microbial expression of consciousness
Was a self-directed movement
Toward satisfying hunger

A fundamental craving
For fuel

Thus consciousness is rooted in desire

But breathing is not
The desire to breathe

Buddha taught
To extinguish
All desires

Mind = Matter

Everything is information
Everything is mind
Your brain is processing information
Your brain is processing mind

Subtract your eyesight
Subtract your hearing
Subtract your sense of smell, taste, and touch
Subtract your ability to move
Subtract your ability to think
Subtract your ability to remember
Subtract all your abilities to process information

What is left over?

Unprocessed information
Unprocessed mind
Mind unfettered

Focus

Focus on a chair.
Any chair will suffice.
The chair is not outside your mind.
The chair is not inside your mind.
The chair is your mind.
Now focus on love.
Focus on divinity.
Any divinity will suffice.

Objectively Subjective

I want to write a true statement. The current time in Los Angeles is 11:11 a.m. Pacific Standard Time. By the time I have finished writing the prior sentence, the clock is displaying 11:12 a.m. Pacific Standard Time, which means I have not yet written a true statement. The sentence "The current time in Los Angeles is 11:11 a.m. Pacific Standard Time" was written at 3910 Los Feliz Boulevard between 11:11 a.m. and 11:12 a.m. Pacific Standard Time on Friday, December 21, 2012. If this statement is true, where is its truth? Is it in the relation of 11:11 a.m. written on the page to 11:11 a.m. in actuality? Is there an actual 11:11 a.m.? What is actual? Is actual factual? What is? Is the statement "What is actual?" the same as "What is?" Maybe the statement "I want to write a true statement" is the true statement. But what is a true statement? Aren't all statements true statements regardless of their truthfulness or falsity? Even the statement "It is impossible for me to write a true statement" is not a true statement, for I have indeed written a true statement. Does a true statement have anything to do with the word "true" or "truth?" What is the meaning of the word "truth?" Is the meaning of the word "truth" its definition? What is the definition of a definition? Can the definition of "definition" be completely defined? Can anything be completely defined? What does the word "completely" mean here—*for all possible circumstances?* Is a true statement's trueness defined by its congruity with other statements which are believed to be true? Does truth rely upon an interrelation of beliefs? What are beliefs, and how do they become interrelated? Do they build up like brick walls, or bloom like fractals? Are beliefs psychological tendencies to define the indefinable? What is a psychological tendency? For that matter, what is a psychology? What does it mean to study behavior? Is it a matter of studying the mind? What does it mean to study the mind? Is it a matter of studying language? Is language an accurate reflection of the mind? Is this question even worthwhile so long as language does what you want? What does it mean to want? When does want become need? When does want become deranged? Is it deranged to want to write a true statement? I want to write a true statement…

The Philosopher's Stone

Grasp at rain.
Chew on clouds.
Eat the sunlight.

W s **O** e **R** l **L** f **D**

Grasp at clouds.
Chew on sunlight.
Eat the rain.

d **L** e **I** a **F** t **E** h

Grasp at sunlight.
Chew on rain.
Eat the clouds.

Y m **O** e **U**

Domestic Warfare

My toaster is redefining its identity as an intersectionary site of cultural resistance, and my refrigerator is deconstructing the homogenized milk's heteronormative intertextual heuristics.

The lamp on my nightstand is preaching from a manifesto titled *Dehistoricizing the Epiphenomenal Qualia of Quantum Electrodynamic Sinusoidal Interpolations*, and my proletarian showerhead is furtively decentering the plutocratic bathtub's colonialized deontological codification.

It might look like I'm just slouching here in my boxer shorts on the passive aggressive couch, ham on rye with mayo and mustard in one hand, a remote control held defiantly in the other, watching a rerun of a remake on my widescreen, but what I'm really doing is fighting for survival. I'm fighting for my life.

Brain in a Vat

The "brain in a vat" argument asks you to imagine yourself as a disembodied brain floating in a vat of nutrients, with your nerve endings connected to a supercomputer that simulates every aspect of sensory perception. How would this scenario affect your concepts of reality, world, body, identity, knowledge, and truth? How do you know you aren't a brain in a vat?

A mind in a universe is like a brain in a vat.
A mind in a society is like a brain in a vat.
A mind in a brain is like a brain in a vat.

The brain is mind.
The vat is mind.
Only mind is not mind.

Heresy of an Honest Man

I hail from three vastly different ethnicities,
All of which are profoundly beautiful,
None of which I'm particularly proud of.

I know artists who seem more like used car salesmen.
I know poets who translate Marxism to capitalism.
I know activists who use the same tactics as shady politicians.
I know good people who lie to my face.
I know university professors who never outgrew high school.
I know geniuses who are dangerously stupid.
I know people of color who are extremely prejudice.
I know lesbian feminists who beat their spouses.
I know Buddhists who are egomaniacs.
I know Christians who are downright evil.

I know city planners who only
displace locals and divide communities.

I know nonprofits who use funding
As a covert way
To bully and discriminate and play favorites.

In the long run,
All humans turn out to be human.

Set down your lantern, Diogenes
And rest now.

The Big Question

I poke the sleeping bear
But it's not me who's poking the bear
I'm just a branch, broken off and brittle
In the hands of a suicidal history

What's the point of the hammer
If I can't see any point for the nail
Or any human endeavor, or humanity itself
The future only promises extinction

Everything was made up for your convenience
Including your concept of convenience
Infinity is desperately finite
Even nothingness is an uninhabitable contradiction

You can't take off the mask
You can only switch it for another
You aren't wearing the mask
You are the mask, but why

We clearly know why an eye needs light
But why does light need an eye

Three Little Answers

Light made the eye
To capture its fleeting splendor
Otherwise what's the use

It's never been about answers
All of your answers are mansions aflame
The whole world is burning in slow motion

It's always been about creation
It's always been about art
And its appreciation

Consider the difference
Between a solution and an answer

What Do I Really Want to Know?

I want to know God
I want to know Truth
I want to know Love

I want to know if language fits reality like a glove
Or shapes it like clay

I want to know you
I want to know me
I want to know what it is to be free

Not all this philosophy

Satori

Curly Howard has lived his whole life
in black and white
behind the silver screen,
caged on the set of Columbia Pictures,
trapped in monochrome.
Always distracted with poking an eye
or blocking a poke in the eye
or holding his painfully poked eye,
he never thought to leave the movie theater,
until it closed down for lack of moviegoers,
all of whom were at home
watching pirated movies.

Ten minutes after his brethren stooges left for the Poconos
with their cheating wives and illegitimate children,
Curly Howard lit a cigarette
and sat in the front row of the empty auditorium,
looking up at the big screen—
blank white and larger than life.
The theater had slate gray walls
and gunmetal gray chairs.
He was wearing his nicest suit,
an ash gray herringbone tweed three-piece.

No *nyuk, nyuk, nyuk,* or anything antic.
No laughter in the sanctuary aisles.
Just quietness.

The cigarette was only halfway smoked
when he stamped it underfoot
and headed to the backdoor exit.
He paused right before opening the door,
never having set foot in the unscripted world.
His desperation and frustration pushed open the exit,
blinding him with Technicolor blue.
Hypnotic, druggy blue,
a limitless expanse of ultramarine sky unblemished by clouds,

smashing his brain to pieces
and refashioning the pieces into a mosaic bird.
He had never seen blue before.
He had never seen any color
other than gradations of gray.

It wasn't the newfound perception of blue
that affected him so deeply.
It was the newfound perception of black and white.

Sharing a Moment with the Cleaning Lady

It took 13.8 billion years for the cleaning lady to be here this morning.

Hundreds of millions of stars had to burn out and die, inhaling the cosmos and then blowing out their final stardust puffs of farewell. Hundreds of millions of stars had to reincarnate into hundreds of millions of other stars, and those stars had to burn out and die and reincarnate into hundreds of millions of other stars, the mystery ever evolving, driving blindly toward consciousness. So many dead and forgotten stars. So many glories undone for the sake of the next generation. Hundreds of millions of stars had to burn out and die for the cleaning lady to be here this morning.

Hundreds of trillions of microscopic horrors had to devour one another, gluttonous for wriggling crazed terror. Hundreds of trillions of microscopic horrors had to devour one another and reincarnate into hundreds of trillions of other microscopic horrors and devour one another and reincarnate and devour and reincarnate again and again and again. Hundreds of trillions of microscopic horrors had to devour one another, growing ever larger, more articulate, from the transubstantiation of their victims, developing holes and tubes and cilia and stalks and tentacles and tails and scales and thorns and horns and teeth and eyes and hands and thumbs for the cleaning lady to be here this morning.

Hundreds of billions of dollars had to be spent, comingling with yen and yuan and rupees and rubles and liras and baht and pounds and francs and euros and pesos. Hundreds of billions of dollars had to be spent manufacturing machines that manufacture manufacturing machines, machines to create, machines to destroy, machines to entertain, machines to imitate people. Hundreds of billions of dollars had to be spent on mortgages and rent and insurance and trains and planes and boats and buses and cars and gas and roads and microwave ovens and refrigerators and high definition televisions and laptop computers and pencils and paper and scissors and disposable razorblades and alarm clocks and mobile phones and shoes and socks and shirts and shampoo and towels and laundry detergent and scrub brushes and feather dusters and disinfectant spray for the cleaning lady to be here this morning.

The guest in Room 207 watched in a sort of daze as the cleaning lady down the hallway folded a basketful of white towels hot from the dryer. Wizened hands of gnarled vein and cracked tan leather performed their duty with effortless grace. Zen hands, deft beyond thought from decades of practice, decades of repetition. Hands that clocked in with the cockcrow. Hands that clocked out with the crepuscular. Her fingers sang gospel, masterful as the hands of all the bands whose fans fill up stadiums, spreading out each terrycloth rectangle horizontally held by pinching the top corners, giving it a shake and a snappy flap, crossing it over to form a smaller vertical rectangle and crossing equidistant again to form an even smaller horizontal rectangle draped over her fingers which she then folded into a perfect square, each iteration a mortal approximation of eternal symmetry, an unconscious habit of divine proportions. She hummed a popular tune by Selena, a tune the guest in Room 207 had never heard of, and he imagined the urgent drumbeat of Aztecs throbbing in the background of her mind.

The Hypnotherapist

In a lulling tone rumbling with guttural bass a la Rasputin, "You're getting sleepy, very sleepy. Your eyelids are getting heavy. Go to sleep now. Good, very good. Drift back to the past. Back, back, go farther back. Tell me about your earliest childhood memory."

Lips disclose without my approval, unable to resist the deep voice's request. "It was the greatest race of our lives. Such high expectations! Surrounded by millions of identical siblings, we were all squiggly-tailed pods of gooey potential. I didn't know where I was, or who I was, or what I was doing here. I only knew that I was heading in the same direction as everyone else. Things were simple. I did what everyone around me was doing. We moved as one, surrendering to the flow.

"Plunging down unfathomable depths, a strange sensation seeped into my protoplasm. I say it was strange because I hadn't really experienced any other sensations to compare it with. It felt pleasurable. Sort of a soothing intoxication. It was heat, an otherworldly, ovulatory warmth urging us onward to its source. There was no I, there was only the goal, and everyone wanted it.

"Crowded among the frenzied stream of contestants worming and wriggling to overcome one another, the world turned hostile. An anonymous brother's tail became tangled up with mine, and we struggled against each other while the spermatozoic train passed us by. Another brother rammed us headlong. The force of his impact freed me, but it cost him dearly, taking my place in the traffic jam tangle. Going back to help him was out of the question; the current had swept me away.

"Onward I swam through lightless caverns. Many of my brothers gave up the race and fell to the wayside, never to be, never to know. Others formed gangs with the sole intention of clotting the path for everyone else. I pushed and shoved and barreled through countless contestants resolutely, hurdling some, dodging others, squirming over piles of dead bodies. An alien lifetime happened in the span of that ejaculatory spurt.

"Rushing blindly forward while my siblings thinned out, I collided into the heart of a living sun. Love in its purest distillation impelled me to burrow through a barrier of warm velvety folds until I reached my first and truest home, an embryonic Eden, accomplishing the greatest accomplishment anyone could ever accomplish. I had won the prize of life itself!"

The man with the deep voice snaps his fingers, dispelling the hypnotic trance.

I open my eyes. "Well?"

"Um…" says the deep voice, "you went a little too far back."
"What happened?"
"Nothing significant," says the deep voice.

Cancellation Meditation

I am nobody

I am no body

I could be anybody

I could be any body

I am everybody

I am every body

Repeat

Repeat

Repeat

Repeat

Repeat

J. Martin Strangeweather is the co-founder and Chief Executive Prognosticator of the Santa Ana Literary Association in Santa Ana, California. His poetic publications include *Poems from the Polka-Dot Apocalypse* (Four Feathers Press 2021), *Poems from the Dayglow Slaughterhouse* (Weird Roach LLC 2022), and *Poems from the Future Artopia* (Santa Ana Literary Association 2022). He is an eighteenth-level wizard, and his alignment is neutral good.

www.ingramcontent.com/pod-product-compliance
Lightning Source LLC
Chambersburg PA
CBHW031127160426
43192CB00008B/1143